Cornerstones of Freedom

The Story of

The Constitution

Marilyn Prolman

CHILDRENS PRESS®
CHICAGO

Library of Congress Cataloging-in-Publication Data

Prolman, Marilyn.
    The Constitution / by Marilyn Prolman.
       p. cm.—(Cornerstones of freedom)
    Originally published: The story of the Constitution.
    Chicago: Childrens Press, 1969.
Summary: Describes the need for unification in a growing
country and discusses the problems and decisions of the men
who drafted the Constitution of the United States.
    ISBN 0-516-06692-7
    1. United States—Constitutional history—Juvenile literature.
2. United States—Constitutional law—Juvenile literature.
[1. United States—Constitutional history. 2. United States—
Constitution.] I. Prolman, Marilyn. Story of the Constitution.
II. Title. III. Series.
KF4541.Z9P77 1995
342.73'029—dc20
[347.30229]   94-35657
                                                          CIP
                                                          AC

On July 8, 1776, the big iron bell in the tower in Philadelphia rang out. The bell announced that the Declaration of Independence had been signed. This historic document stated: "These united colonies are, and of a right ought to be, free and independent states."

Signing the Declaration of Independence was only one step on a long, hard road to real independence. In 1776, the thirteen American

Ringing the Liberty Bell in Philadelphia

colonies were fighting to break free from the rule of Great Britain. After the Declaration of Independence was signed, the Revolutionary War continued until the new United States finally won the war in 1783.

During the war, the colonies worked together because they were fighting for a common cause. After the war was won, the thirteen states set up governments that were very different from each other. Each state made its own money. Each had its own way of taxing. The people referred to themselves as "New Yorkers," "Virginians," or "Pennsylvanians" rather than as "Americans." They were not yet truly united.

In 1781, the thirteen states had agreed to adopt the Articles of Confederation. This document mapped out a bold, new experiment in government in which people made the laws of the nation. Most other countries were ruled by kings. The idea of people making their own laws was brand new.

The Articles of Confederation created a nation in which each state held a lot of power, and the national government held comparatively little. There was not even a president to lead the nation. In the 1780s, the American people shared a general fear of a large, all-powerful government ruling their lives. They had just fought a revolution to win their independence from years of dominance by the king of England. So the newly

King George III of England ruled the colonies until Americans won their independence in the American Revolution. The Americans were then determined to create a government in which no king or all-powerful ruler could take over the country.

freed Americans created a small national government, which limped along for several years. It proved to be extremely inefficient.

In this government, Congress could pass laws for the nation, but it had no way of enforcing those laws. For instance, the country needed to pay off the debt it had accumulated during the Revolution, but the states refused to contribute to this effort. The individual states even made their own treaties with American Indian tribes and European nations. When the Articles of Confederation went into effect, it was as if the United States became thirteen separate countries.

The biggest problem during the years under the Articles of Confederation centered on money. Each state printed its own money, so business dealings between states were difficult. For instance, a Virginia farmer selling cotton would want to receive only Virginia money in return. Currency from other states might be worthless in Virginia. This meant he probably would not do business with anyone from outside Virginia. Some states also placed taxes on goods that were brought in from other states.

The problems came to a violent head when a Massachusetts farmer named Daniel Shays led a revolt against the government of Massachusetts in 1786. Shays' Rebellion alerted the nation to the desperate need for a stronger central

Examples of different currencies used in New York (right) and New Jersey (left)

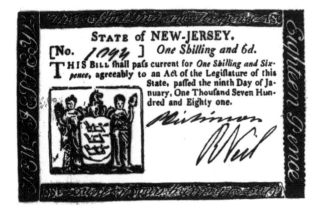

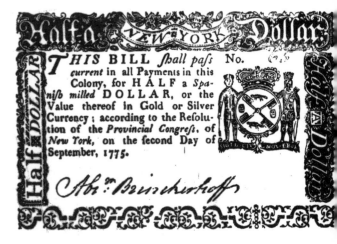

Violence breaks out during Shays' Rebellion of 1786.

government. If the current system continued, the entire country might fall into revolution all over again. The Annapolis Convention was called in 1786 to discuss the problem. There, representatives of five states called for a national convention to occur the following year in Philadelphia. They believed all thirteen states needed to solve the problems caused by the Articles of Confederation.

On May 25, 1787, the Constitutional Convention began in Philadelphia, Pennsylvania. Rhode Island was the only state that refused to send delegates—it did not want a national government interfering in its state affairs. So fifty-five delegates representing the twelve other states entered the Philadelphia State House on May 25. And what an amazing group of patriots they were!

George Washington, retired general of the Revolutionary Army, came to the convention from his Mount Vernon plantation. Washington was still one of the most influential men in American politics, and he would eventually become the nation's first president. Benjamin

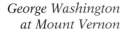

George Washington at Mount Vernon

James Madison

Franklin already lived in Philadelphia, so he didn't have to travel far to attend. At age eighty-one, Franklin still had the active and creative mind of a young man. Thirty-six-year-old James Madison was still a young man, but his diligent work at the convention would earn him the unofficial title, "Father of the Constitution." Madison eventually wrote *Notes on the Federal Convention,* which provides historians centuries later with a full report on what happened at the convention.

Other key players at the convention included such famous patriots as Robert Morris, a rich man who had donated a fortune to help finance the Revolutionary Army; Oliver Ellsworth, a famous lawyer, who later became chief justice of the Supreme Court; Roger Sherman, the only man to sign the Articles of Association, the Declaration of Independence, the Articles of Confederation, and the Constitution; and Gouverneur Morris, a leading politician, who spoke more often at the convention than any other delegate—173 times in all!

When the meeting began, George Washington was quickly elected president of the convention. After only brief discussion, it became clear to everyone that the Articles of Confederation would not survive. The focus of the convention shifted from fixing the Articles to creating a completely new plan for government.

The delegates agreed on one basic point: they wanted a new, efficient government that would protect the individual rights of all U.S. citizens.

Benjamin Franklin discusses the Constitution at his Philadelphia home.

But designing such a government proved extremely difficult. There were many key issues on which the delegates disagreed.

For instance, New York delegate Alexander Hamilton wanted the president and legislators to be elected for life. Other delegates argued that such a situation would be too much like being ruled by a king. Most of these men had recently fought the Revolutionary War to break

Alexander Hamilton was a vocal delegate at the convention and one of the most outspoken politicians of his day. He went on to serve in George Washington's administration as the first secretary of the treasury.

free from the rule of the king of England. The delegates agreed that no all-powerful ruler (or dictator) should ever be allowed to take over the United States. So as they designed the new government, the delegates were careful to protect against one part of the government gaining too much power.

The delegates also agreed that the citizens of the United States should be involved in making the country's laws. The most efficient way to do this is to have the people elect representatives to express the people's opinions in Congress. But here, the delegates reached a roadblock. The large states wanted more representatives in Congress than the small states, and the small states wanted equal representation in Congress. Arguments on this point grew heated, and tempers flared as the hot summer days dragged on.

Roger Sherman

On July 16, the convention finally solved this disagreement with what has become known as the "Great Compromise," which was designed mainly by delegates Oliver Ellsworth and Roger Sherman. The plan divided the Congress into two parts, which satisfied both the small and large states. The smaller states would be equally represented in the Senate, where every state, no matter how small, was given two senators. The large states would hold more influence in the House of Representatives, where states with larger populations were given more representa-

Oliver Ellsworth

The Great Compromise led to the establishment of a two-part Congress. In the House of Representatives (top), states with larger populations have more representatives than smaller states. In the Senate (bottom), every state has two senators.

tives. By designing these new, separate houses of Congress, the delegates hurdled the greatest obstacle of the convention.

After seven months of intensive work, the framework for a new government was complete. Pennsylvania delegate Gouverneur Morris was named to head a committee that would do the actual writing of the Constitution. In the end, the Constitution that Morris wrote turned out to be one of the most influential documents in world history.

Gouverneur Morris

The Constitution begins with a long sentence, called the preamble, which states exactly why the new government was being formed:

We the People of the United States, in order to form a more perfect Union, establish justice, insure domestic tranquility, provide for the common defence, promote the general welfare, and secure the blessings of liberty to ourselves and our posterity, do ordain and establish this Constitution for the United States of America.

The preamble basically says that the delegates wanted the states to exist in a friendly manner and to be able to do business easily and profitably—this, they called domestic tranquillity. They also wanted the country to be able to defend itself from foreign invasion. And they wanted to secure liberty for themselves and their children. The next seven articles of the Constitution would explain exactly how the new U.S. government would accomplish these lofty goals.

Article I of the Constitution explains the legislative branch of the government, which is headed by Congress. The primary responsibility of Congress is to make the laws for the nation. The Constitution gives Congress many

The two bodies of Congress meet at the U.S. Capitol.

responsibilities, including the powers to levy taxes on the nation, to maintain a military to defend the nation, to coin money, and even to set the country's standards of weights and measures.

Article II defines the executive branch, which is headed by the president. It is the president's responsibility to make sure the laws of Congress are enforced. The president is allowed to veto any bill passed by Congress, thus preventing it from becoming law.

In Article III, the Constitution defines the judicial branch of government. This branch consists of the court system, which is headed by the Supreme Court. The main responsibility

President Bill Clinton at his desk in the Oval Office of the White House. The president is in charge of the executive branch of the government.

The Supreme Court Building in Washington, D.C. The Supreme Court is the highest court in the country and heads the judicial branch of government.

of the judicial branch is to interpret, or explain, the laws of Congress and the Constitution. The Supreme Court today consists of nine justices who are appointed for life terms by the president.

These first three articles spell out the separation of powers in the new government. The delegates wanted to ensure that no single branch of government could grab too much power, so a system of "checks and balances" was designed. This means that each branch can overrule certain decisions of the other branches.

For instance, the president has power over Congress because he can veto Congress's bills. But Congress can override the president's veto if it votes to pass the bill by a two-thirds majority.

Also, the president must have the permission (or the "advice and consent") of the Senate to appoint a person to the Supreme Court or to make a treaty with a nation. Many other such checks are built into the government. These checks ensure that the branches work within the boundaries of the Constitution.

Once this form of divided government was agreed upon, the delegates wrote four more articles. Article IV explains how each state must honor the laws of all the states. It also says that the national government shall protect each state against invasion and violence. Article V explains that the Constitution can be amended if the amendment is agreed upon by a three-fourths majority of the nation. Article VI officially states that the Constitution is the "supreme law of the land." It also explains how the government will perform such tasks as paying national debts and making treaties. Finally, Article VII states that the new Constitution would be ratified when nine of the thirteen states voted in favor of it.

The hot summer of 1787 drew to a close. Gouverneur Morris carefully wrote out the document by hand. On September 17, 1787, it was signed by thirty-nine of the delegates. Although the Constitution is a symbol of agreement, several delegates still were unhappy with the document. Some refused to sign the Constitution because they thought it gave the national government too much power over the states.

The delegates who did agree signed in geographical order, from north to south— New Hampshire's delegates signing first, and Georgia's signing last. The delegates signed their names with a quill pen dipped in the same silver inkwell that was used eleven years earlier to sign the Declaration of Independence.

Left: The inkstand used to sign the Constitution
Above: A ledger page on which George Washington wrote down each state's votes on different constitutional issues

In September 1787, a new government was created when the Constitution was signed. But before this government could begin operating, the Constitution had to be ratified by nine of the thirteen states. The individual states called meetings to discuss the new Constitution. Through months of even more heated argument, several states came aboard in favor of the Constitution. New Hampshire became the ninth state to vote for ratification on June 21, 1788. The Constitution was officially adopted, and plans were made to start the government.

After the Constitution was ratified by nine states, the new U.S. government began operating. In 1789, George Washington became the nation's first president when he took the oath of office.

In 1789, the first U.S. Senate convened in New York City, which was the nation's capital at the time.

But the debates still continued. People believed that, for the sake of national unity, it would be best if all thirteen states (rather than just a majority) voted in favor of the Constitution. Because many people still thought it did not provide enough protection of people's individual liberties, several states refused to ratify the Constitution unless it was changed. The document was barely a year old, and amendments to alter it already were being written.

When the first Congress met in March 1789, James Madison proposed fifteen amendments to the Constitution. Hundreds of days of debate followed, and ten of the amendments finally were ratified on December 15, 1791. These first ten amendments were called the Bill of Rights because they dealt mostly with individuals' rights—such as people's rights to freedom of religion, speech, and peaceful assembly. In the two centuries that have followed, fifteen more amendments have been added to the Constitution. With the passage of the Bill of Rights almost everyone's concerns were satisfied, and the Constitution finally was adopted by all the states.

Congress OF THE United States,

begun and held at the City of New-York, on

Wednesday the Fourth of March, one thousand seven hundred and eighty nine.

THE Conventions of a number of the States, having at the time of their adopting the Constitution, expressed a desire, in order to prevent misconstruction or abuse of its powers, that further declaratory and restrictive clauses should be added: And as extending the ground of public confidence in the Government, will best ensure the beneficent ends of its institution

RESOLVED by the Senate and House of Representatives of the United States of America, in Congress assembled, two thirds of both Houses concurring, that the following Articles be proposed to the Legislatures of the several States, as amendments to the Constitution of the United States, all, or any of which Articles, when ratified by three fourths of the said Legislatures, to be valid to all intents and purposes, as part of the said Constitution; viz.

ARTICLES in addition to, and amendment of the Constitution of the United States of America, proposed by Congress, and ratified by the Legislatures of the several States, pursuant to the fifth Article of the original Constitution.

Article the first. After the first enumeration required by the first Article of the Constitution, there shall be one Representative for every thirty thousand, until the number shall amount to one hundred, after which, the proportion shall be so regulated by Congress, that there shall be not less than one hundred Representatives, nor less than one Representative for every forty thousand persons, until the number of Representatives shall amount to two hundred, after which the proportion shall be so regulated by Congress, that there shall not be less than two hundred Representatives, nor more than one Representative for every fifty thousand persons.

Article the second. No law, varying the compensation for the services of the Senators and Representatives, shall take effect, until an election of Representatives shall have intervened.

Article the third. Congress shall make no law respecting an establishment of religion, or prohibiting the free exercise thereof; or abridging the freedom of speech, or of the press; or the right of the people peaceably to assemble, and to petition the Government for a redress of grievances.

Article the fourth. A well regulated militia, being necessary to the security of a free State, the right of the people to keep and bear arms, shall not be infringed.

Article the fifth. No Soldier shall, in time of peace be quartered in any house, without the consent of the owner, nor in time of war, but in a manner to be prescribed by law.

Article the sixth. The right of the people to be secure in their persons, houses, papers, and effects, against unreasonable searches and seizures, shall not be violated, and no Warrants shall issue, but upon probable cause, supported by Oath or affirmation, and particularly describing the place to be searched, and the persons or things to be seized.

Article the seventh. No person shall be held to answer for a capital, or otherwise infamous crime, unless on a presentment or indictment of a Grand jury, except in cases arising in the land or naval forces, or in the Militia, when in actual service in time of War or public danger; nor shall any person be subject for the same offence to be twice put in jeopardy of life or limb; nor shall be compelled in any criminal case to be a witness against himself, nor be deprived of life, liberty, or property, without due process of law; nor shall private property be taken for public use, without just compensation.

Article the eighth. In all criminal prosecutions, the accused shall enjoy the right to a speedy and public trial, by an impartial jury of the State and district wherein the crime shall have been committed, which district shall have been previously ascertained by law, and to be informed of the nature and cause of the accusation; to be confronted with the witnesses against him; to have compulsory process for obtaining witnesses in his favor, and to have the assistance of counsel for his defence.

Article the ninth. In suits at common law, where the value in controversy shall exceed twenty dollars, the right of trial by jury shall be preserved, and no fact tried by a jury, shall be otherwise re-examined in any Court of the United States, than according to the rules of the common law.

Article the tenth. Excessive bail shall not be required, nor excessive fines imposed, nor cruel and unusual punishments inflicted.

Article the eleventh. The enumeration in the Constitution, of certain rights, shall not be construed to deny or disparage others retained by the people.

Article the twelfth. The powers not delegated to the United States by the Constitution, nor prohibited by it to the States, are reserved to the States respectively, or to the people.

ATTEST,

Frederick Augustus Muhlenberg, Speaker of the House of Representatives

John Adams, Vice-President of the United States, and President of the Senate.

John Beckley, Clerk of the House of Representatives.

Sam. A. Otis Secretary of the Senate.

The Bill of Rights, adopted in 1791, contains the first ten amendments to the Constitution.

AMENDMENTS TO THE CONSTITUTION
The first ten amendments were adopted as the Bill of Rights in 1791; the other amendments were adopted in the years listed.

Free Press

Amendment 1
Restricts the government from infringing on individuals' rights to religion, free speech, free assembly; establishes freedom of the press.

Amendment 2
Establishes individuals' right to bear arms (own weapons).

Ownership of handguns is protected by 2nd Amendment.

Amendment 3
Restricts the government from forcing individuals to turn over their homes to soldiers, which had been a problem during the Revolution.

Police Search

Amendment 4
Protects individuals against unlawful searches by legal authorities (police).

Amendments 5, 6, 7, 8
Establish the rights of persons accused of crimes during their arrest and trial.

Amendment 9
Ensures that all individual rights are protected, even if some are not specifically spelled out in the Bill of Rights.

Amendment 10
States that any powers not given to the national government will be given to the individual states.

Amendment 11—1795
Establishes that a citizen of one state cannot sue another state.

Amendment 12—1804
Revises the electoral college system of electing a president and vice president.

Amendment 13—1865
Abolishes the right of individuals to own slaves.

Amendment 14—1868
Declares that the states cannot infringe on the civil rights and citizenship of any individuals.

Amendment 15—1870
Declares that states may not deny any citizen the right to vote because of race.

African American voting in the 1800s

Income-tax Clerk

Amendment 16—1913
Establishes the government's right to collect income taxes from individuals.

Amendment 17—1913
Gives the people of each state the right to elect their senators.

Amendment 18—1919
Outlaws the production, sale, or transportation of liquor.

Women protesting for the right to vote

Amendment 19—1920
Gives women the right to vote.

Amendment 20—1933
Declares that new presidents and members of Congress will take office soon after they are elected.

Amendment 21—1933
Repeals the 18th Amendment, thus making it legal to sell liquor.

Legalization of Liquor

Amendment 22—1951
Limits a president to two terms in office.

Amendment 23—1961
Gives citizens of Washington, D.C., the right to vote in presidential elections.

Amendment 24—1964
Declares that the government cannot charge a "poll tax" to voters, which previously had made it impossible for some poor people to vote.

Amendment 25—1967
Defines who will take over an office if a president or vice president dies or leaves office before his or her term ends.

Amendment 26—1971
Gives voting rights to anyone eighteen years old or older.

Amendment 27—1992
Regulates pay raises for members of Congress.

An eighteen-year-old voting

If the men who met at the Constitutional Convention were alive today, they would no doubt be proud of the results of their work. Democracy in the United States has become the form of government that is most often copied around the world. Since the 1700s, numerous revolutions have been fought in other countries. From the French Revolution of the 1790s to the collapse of the communist Soviet Union in 1991, new nations have been formed on all continents. Many of these new governments have used as a model the system outlined in the United States Constitution.

Perhaps the secret to the success of the Constitutional Convention was the delegates' unshakable faith in the future. As Gouverneur Morris said, "Surely those who come after us will judge better of things present, than we can judge of things future."

The 1990s present an entirely different world than that of the 1770s. Computers, telephones, satellite communications, nuclear weapons, and modern medicine create conditions that the delegates could not have imagined in 1787. Nevertheless, the basic principles set forth in the United States Constitution still guide the nation as every new age dawns.

GLOSSARY

amend – to change a previous agreement or document; twenty-seven amendments have been made to the Constitution

article – each of the seven sections of the Constitution are called "articles"

convention – a formal gathering or meeting of people for a particular purpose; the Constitution was written at the Constitutional Convention of 1787

compromise – an agreement reached when two sides each give up certain demands

currency – a form of money

debt – money that is owed to another party

delegate – a person who acts and speaks for a larger group

Currency

patriot – a person loyal to his or her country and willing to fight for the right to remain there

preamble – the introduction to the Constitution

quill – a bird's feather used as a pen

ratify – to support an idea; to approve of in an official way

Revolutionary War – The war between Great Britain and the American colonies (1775–1783) in which Americans won their independence

separation of powers – the system of government in which the power rests in three separate branches (legislative, executive, and judicial)

taxes – money paid by citizens to a government

tranquillity – freedom from trouble and disturbance; peacefulness

treaty – agreement between two or more nations that concerns trade or ends a war

Quill

veto – to reject; for a congressional bill to become law, the president must agree to it — if he disagrees, he can "veto" it, or refuse to sign it

TIMELINE

	1775
Declaration of Independence signed	**1776**
Articles of Confederation ratified	**1781**
	1783
Shays' Rebellion; Annapolis Convention	**1786**
	1787
New Hampshire ratifies Constitution	**1788**
March 4: First Congress meets	**1789**
	1791
April 30: George Washington inaugurated as first president	**1812** **1815**
	1861
13th Amendment (abolishes slavery)	**1865**

} Revolutionary War

1791 Bill of Rights ratified

May 25:
Constitutional
Convention
begins

July 16:
The Great
Compromise

September 17:
Constitution
signed

} War of 1812

} Civil War

19th Amendment
(gives women
the right to vote)

	1913
World War I {	**1914**
	1918
	1919
	1920
	1929
	1933
	1939
	1945
Korean War {	**1950**
	1953
	1971

1913 16th Amendment (income tax)

1919 18th Amendment (outlaws liquor)

1929 The Great Depression begins
1933 21st Amendment (repeals 18th Amendment)

} World War II

1971 26th Amendment
(gives eighteen-year-olds the right to vote)

INDEX *(Boldface page numbers indicate illustrations.)*

PHOTO CREDITS

Cover, Architect of the Capitol; 1, ©David M. Doody/Tom Stack and Associates; 2, North Wind Picture Archives; 3, Bettmann; 5, North Wind; 6, (both pictures), Bettmann; 7, 8, North Wind; 9, Bettmann; 10, 11, North Wind; 12, 13 (bottom), Bettmann; 13 (top), 14 (both pictures), 15, North Wind; 16, Tom Stack and Associates; 17, ©Cameramann International, Ltd.; 18, Reuters/Bettmann; 19, SuperStock, Inc.; 21 (top), Library of Congress; 21 (bottom), Independence National Historical Park; 22, 23, Bettmann; 25, National Archives; 26 (all photos), 27 (left), AP/Wide World; 27 (right), 28 (top left, center left), Stock Montage, Inc.; 28 (bottom right), UPI/Bettmann; 30 (top), Bettmann; 30 (bottom), Independence National Historical Park; 31 (left), Stock Montage, Inc.; 31 (right), North Wind

ADDITIONAL PICTURE IDENTIFICATIONS

Cover: *"Scene at the Signing of the Consitution,"* a painting by Howard Chandler Christy that is currently on display at the U.S. Capitol.
Page 1: *The Constitution, Bill of Rights, and Declaration of Independence on display at the National Archives Building in Washington, D.C.*
Page 2: *The meeting of President George Washington's first cabinet*

STAFF

Project Editor: Mark Friedman
Design and Electronic Composition: TJS Design
Photo Editor: Jan Izzo
Cornerstones of Freedom Logo: David Cunningham

ABOUT THE AUTHOR

Marilyn Prolman was born in Boston, Massachusetts. She attended the University of Wisconsin, where she majored in English. Ms. Prolman is the author of many books in the Childrens Press *Cornerstones of Freedom* series.